Insect World

Beetles

by Mari Schuh

D1524493

Bullfrog Books

Ideas for Parents and Teachers

Bullfrog Books let children practice nonfiction reading at the earliest reading levels. Repetition, familiar words, and photo labels support early readers.

Before Reading
- Discuss the cover photo. What does it tell them?
- Look at the picture glossary together. Read and discuss the words.

Read the Book
- "Walk" through the book and look at the photos. Let the child ask questions. Point out the photo labels.
- Read the book to the child, or have him or her read independently.

After Reading
- Prompt the child to think more. Ask: Have you ever seen a beetle? How did you know it was a beetle?

Dedicated to Jacob Caruso of Kenosha, Wisconsin
—Mari Schuh

Bullfrog Books are published by Jump!
5357 Penn Avenue South
Minneapolis, MN 55419
www.jumplibrary.com

Library of Congress Cataloging-in-Publication Data
Schuh, Mari C., 1975-
Beetles / by Mari Schuh.
p. cm. -- (Insect world)
Summary: "This photo-illustrated book for early readers tells how to identify beetles and gives examples of different species. Includes picture glossary"--Provided by publisher.
Includes bibliographical references and index.
ISBN 978-1-62031-052-6 (hardcover : alk. paper)
ISBN 978-1-62496-044-4 (ebook)
1. Beetles--Juvenile literature. 2. Beetles--Identification--Juvenile literature. I. Title. II. Series: Schuh, Mari C., 1975- Insect world.
QL576.2.S38 2014
595.76--dc23   2012039936

Series Editor   Rebecca Glaser
Book Designer   Ellen Huber
Photo Researcher   Heather Dreisbach

Photo Credits: 123rf, 7; Dreamstime, cover, 6, 9, 18, 23tl, 20-21; Getty Images, 14-15, 23bl; iStockphoto, 5c, 5f; Shutterstock, 3b, 3t, 5a, 5b, 5d, 5e, 8, 10, 11, 12, 16, 22, 23mr, 23ml, 23tr, 23br; Superstock, 19; Veer, 1, 4, 13, 24

Printed in the United States of America at Corporate Graphics in North Mankato, Minnesota.
4-2013 / P.O. 1003

10 9 8 7 6 5 4 3 2 1

Table of Contents

Lots of Beetles

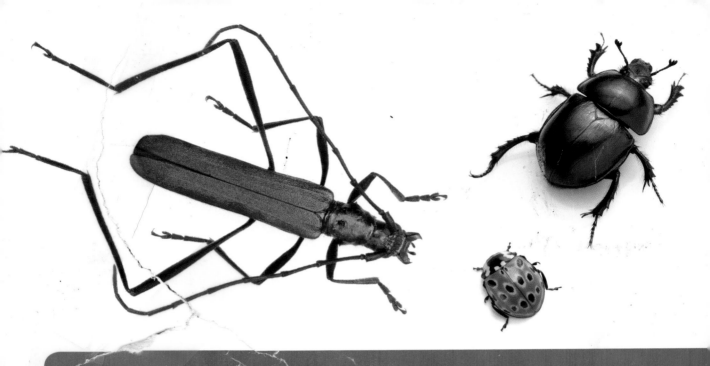

Long and thin. Small and round.
Beetles do not all look the same.
So, what makes an insect a beetle?

hard wings

Beetles have two hard wings.

The hard wings meet in a line.

The hard wings cover two soft wings.

soft wings

jaws

Beetles have jaws.

They chew food.

I am a stag beetle.
I have big jaws.
They help me fight.

I am a ladybug.

I am round.

I am a firefly.
I am a beetle, too.

My thin body glows at night.

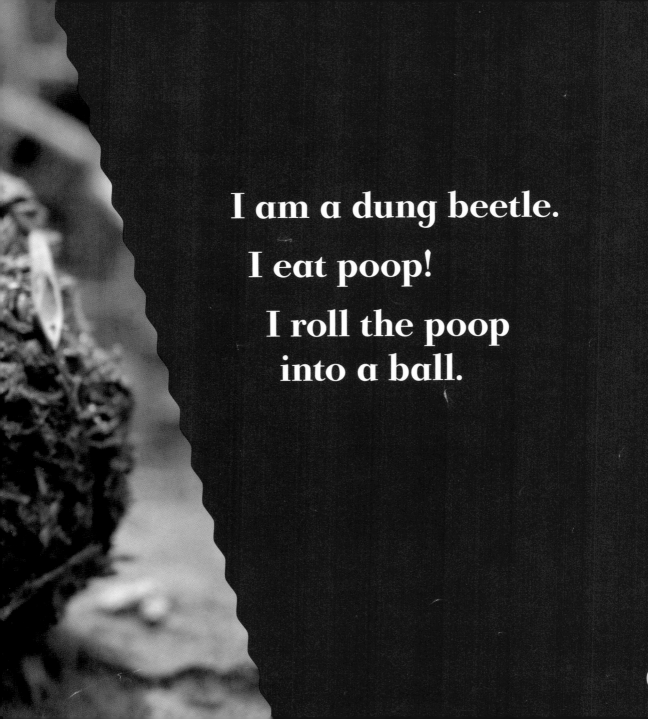

I am a dung beetle.

I eat poop!

I roll the poop
into a ball.

I am a diving beetle.

I eat tiny fish.

I am a tiger beetle.
My long legs make me fast.

Have you
seen a beetle?

Parts of a Beetle

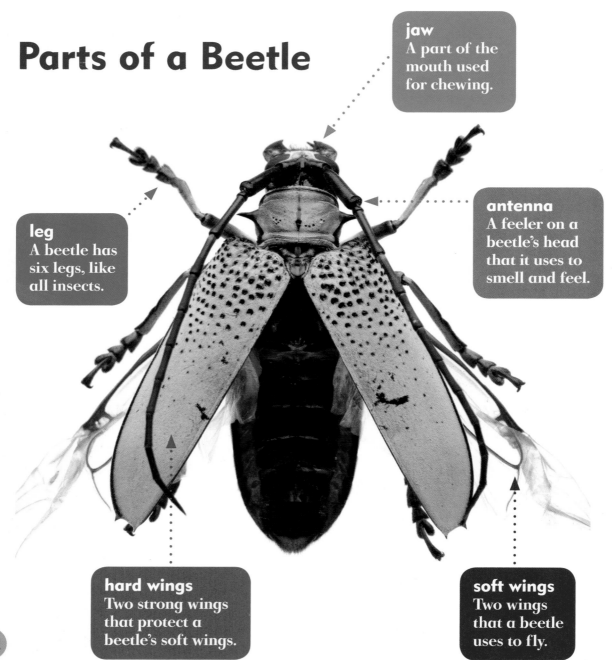

jaw
A part of the mouth used for chewing.

antenna
A feeler on a beetle's head that it uses to smell and feel.

leg
A beetle has six legs, like all insects.

hard wings
Two strong wings that protect a beetle's soft wings.

soft wings
Two wings that a beetle uses to fly.

Picture Glossary

diving beetle
A big, dark beetle that lives in the water.

ladybug
A small, round beetle; many ladybugs have spots.

dung beetle
A beetle that eats animal waste.

stag beetle
A beetle with big, sharp jaws.

firefly
A beetle that makes light in its body so it can find a mate.

tiger beetle
A fast beetle with long, thin legs.

Index

To Learn More

Learning more is as easy as 1, 2, 3.

1) Go to www.factsurfer.com

2) Enter "beetle" into the search box.

3) Click the "Surf" button to see a list of websites.

With factsurfer.com, finding more information is just a click away.